DOWNTOWN DOONESBURY

Doonesbury books by G. B. Trudeau

Still a Few Bugs in the System
The President Is a Lot Smarter Than You Think
But This War Had Such Promise
Call Me When You Find America
Guilty, Guilty, Guilty!
"What Do We Have for the Witnesses, Johnnie?"
Dare To Be Great, Ms. Caucus
Wouldn't a Gremlin Have Been More Sensible?
"Speaking of Inalienable Rights, Amy . . ."
You're Never Too Old for Nuts and Berries
An Especially Tricky People
As the Kid Goes for Broke
Stalking the Perfect Tan
"Any Grooming Hints for Your Fans, Rollie?"
But the Pension Fund Was Just Sitting There
We're Not Out of the Woods Yet
A Tad Overweight, but Violet Eyes to Die For
And That's My Final Offer!
He's Never Heard of You, Either
In Search of Reagan's Brain
Ask for May, Settle for June
Unfortunately, She Was Also Wired for Sound
The Wreck of the "Rusty Nail"
You Give Great Meeting, Sid
Doonesbury: A Musical Comedy
Check Your Egos at the Door
That's *Doctor* Sinatra, You Little Bimbo!
Death of a Party Animal
Downtown Doonesbury

In Large Format

The Doonesbury Chronicles
Doonesbury's Greatest Hits
The People's Doonesbury
Doonesbury Dossier: The Reagan Years

A DOONESBURY BOOK BY
G.B. Trudeau

DOWNTOWN DOONESBURY

AN OWL BOOK · HENRY HOLT AND COMPANY · NEW YORK

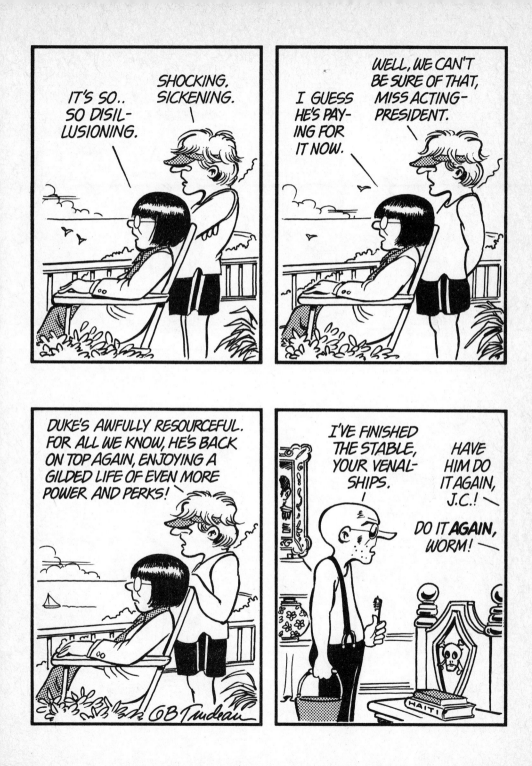

"... DONALD ELLISON, EMBEZZLED BANK FUNDS, IMPRISONED. LEE S. VARNER, DEFRAUDED FEDERAL GOVERNMENT OF $53,500, CONVICTED..."
Hi! Remember me? I'm your boss.
"RICHARD V. ALLEN, ACCEPTED MONEY AND WATCHES, RESIGNED..."
Both of us work for National Public Radio.
Our budget is approved by The White House.
"ED MEESE, AIDED FINANCIALLY BY SIX PERSONS LATER GIVEN FEDERAL JOBS, PROMOTED."
AVOID THE RUSH, FOLKS! CLEAN OUT YOUR DESKS NOW!
get is
ed by
GB Trudeau

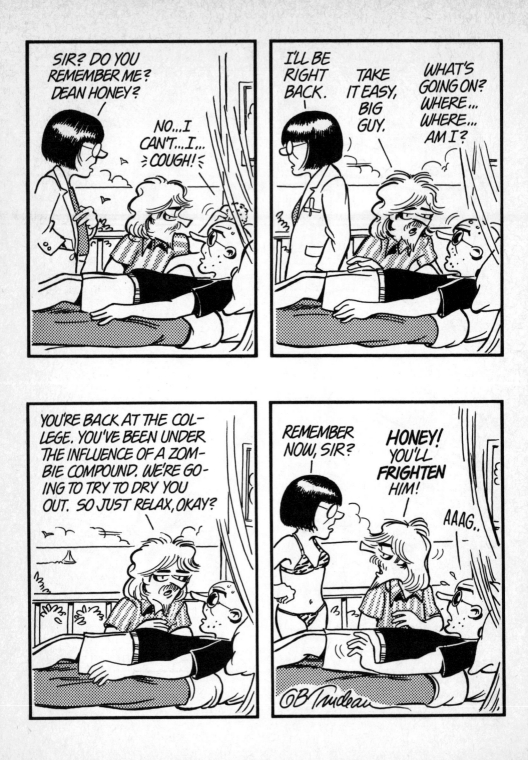

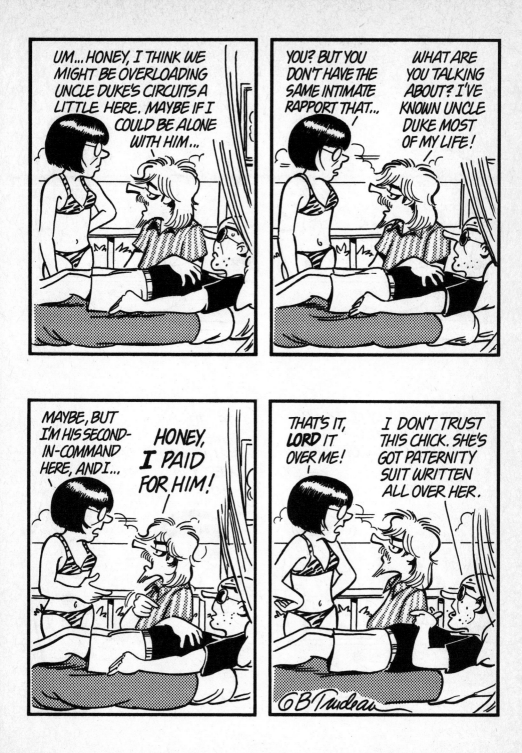

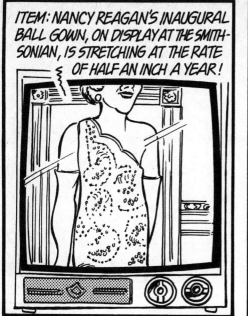

ITEM: NANCY REAGAN'S INAUGURAL BALL GOWN, ON DISPLAY AT THE SMITHSONIAN, IS STRETCHING AT THE RATE OF HALF AN INCH A YEAR!

MUSEUM OFFICIALS SAY IT WILL COST $10,000 TO "STABILIZE" THE HAND-BEADED, WHITE SATIN SHEATH. BUT INCREDIBLY, THE FUNDS ARE NOT AVAILABLE!

NANCY REA

A NATION THAT IS UNABLE TO CHECK THE GROWTH OF A FIRST LADY'S GOWN IS A NATION IN SHAME. JOIN US AS WE EXAMINE THE TRAGIC COST OF A MINDLESS BUDGETARY MECHANISM IN...

©B Trudeau

Guaranteed true!

GRAMM-RUDMAN

HORROR STORIES!

FIRST IN A SERIES...

THE UNCHECKED STRETCHING OF NANCY REAGAN'S INAUGURAL GOWN. AN INCREDIBLE BUT TRUE GRAMM-RUDMAN *HORROR STORY!*

NAN

HERE AT THE SMITHSONIAN'S MUSEUM OF AMERICAN HISTORY, OFFICIALS SAY THE SATIN GALANOS CREATION HAS ALREADY GROWN 2"! BUT THE $10,000 NEEDED TO "STABILIZE" THE GOWN HAS BEEN CUT!

WHAT ARE THE CONSEQUENCES? USING AN ANIMATION SIMULATOR, WE CAN PROJECT WHAT THE GROWING GOWN WILL LOOK LIKE TO A MUSEUM VISITOR IN THE YEAR 2050.

WHETHER HISTORY WILL FORGIVE US REMAINS TO BE SEEN.

©BTrudeau

THE TARMAC WAS SHIMMERING IN THE HEAT AS FLIGHT 307 DISGORGED THE CONGRESSIONAL FACT-FINDING TEAM...

THE TEAM'S MISSION: TO TALK TO CONTRA LEADERS ABOUT $13 MILLION IN MISSING U.S. HUMANITARIAN AID!

...AND WE'LL BE MEETING WITH "EL CADÁVER", "HOMICIDA", AND "COMMANDER LESS-THAN-ZERO."

BUT THIS IS CONTRA COUNTRY, THE ONE CITY WHERE THE NICARAGUAN REBELS ENJOY FULL POPULAR SUPPORT.

YES, MIAMI.

YOU REALLY THINK IT'S ME?

IT'S VERY TAKE CHARGE, COMMANDER!

THIS IS ROLAND HEDLEY. TODAY THE CIA STEPPED OUT INTO THE WARM SUNSHINE OF **OVERT** OPERATIONS.

AT ANDREWS AIR FORCE BASE, TOP "COMPANY" OPERATIVES LEFT ON THEIR MISSION TO DIRECT THE WAR AGAINST NICARAGUA'S SANDINISTAS.

FINALLY FREED FROM THE NEED TO KEEP CIA INVOLVEMENT SECRET, SPOOK SPOUSES TURNED OUT IN DROVES FOR FAREWELL CEREMONIES.

SUSAN, HAS YOUR HUSBAND TOLD YOU HIS CODE NAME?

YES, IT'S "REX." ISN'T THAT THE CUTEST?

EVERYTHING'S CHANGED, REV, EVERYTHING! J.J. AND I DON'T HAVE A SINGLE THING IN COMMON ANYMORE!
AND YET I THINK OF HER CONSTANTLY. I SEE HER FACE EVERYWHERE. EVEN THE WIND SEEMS TO WHISPER HER NAME...
RHODA!
RHODA!
RHODA!
RHODA!
RHODA?
MUST HAVE CHANGED DIRECTIONS.
GLORIA!
BARBI!
©B Trudeau

MIKE, I KNOW YOU THOUGHT THAT J.J. WOULD REMAIN THE SAME SWEET WAIF FOREVER.
BUT PEOPLE DO CHANGE, MIKE. WE HAVE TO ADJUST.
COULD IT BE IT WAS ALL SO SIMPLE THEN?... HAS TIME REWRITTEN EVERY LINE?
SO I... I...
...MISTY, WATER-COLORED MEMORIES... OF THE WAAY WE WERE...
MIKE, COULD YOU TURN DOWN YOUR SOUNDTRACK A LITTLE?
OH... SURE. SORRY.
US MAIL
©B Trudeau